REFERENCES

American Speech-Language-Hearing Association. (2005a). *Evidence-based practice in communication disorders* [Position Statement]. Retrieved from www.asha.org/policy

American Speech-Language-Hearing Association. (2005b). *Roles and responsibilities of speech-language pathologists with respect to augmentative and alternative communication* [Position Statement]. Retrieved from www.asha.org/policy

Cherney, L.R., Halper, A.S., & Burns, M.S. (1996). *Clinical management of right hemisphere dysfunction.* Gaithersburg, MD: Aspen Publishers.

Chomsky, N. (1965). *Aspects of the theory of syntax.* Cambridge, MA: MIT Press.

Gleitman, L. (1990). The structural sources of verb meanings. *Language Acquisition, 1,* 3-55.

Grice, H.P. (1975). Logic and conversation. In P. Cole & J.L. Morgan (Eds.), *Syntax and semantics: Speech acts* (Vol. 3, pp. 41–58). New York: Academic Press.

Hartley, L. (1995). *Cognitive communicative abilities following brain injury.* San Diego, CA: Singular Publishing.

National Joint Committee for the Communicative Needs of Persons with Severe Disabilities. (1992). Guidelines for meeting the communication needs of persons with severe disabilities. *Asha, 34*(Suppl. 7), 2–3.

Oller, D.K. (1980). The emergence of the sounds of speech in infancy. In G. Yeni-Komshian, J. Kavanagh, & C.A. Ferguson (Eds.), *Child phonology: Volume 1. Production* (pp. 93-112). New York: Academic Press.

Peña-Brooks, A., & Hegde, M.N. (2007). *Assessment and treatment of articulation and phonological disorders in children.* Austin, TX: Pro-Ed.

Piaget, J. (1970). *Structuralism.* New York: Basic Books.

Pinker, S. (1989). *Learnability and cognition: The acquisition of argument structure.* Cambridge, MA: MIT Press.

Roseberry-McKibbin, C., & Hegde, M.N. (2006). *An advanced review of speech-language pathology: Preparation for PRAXIS and comprehensive examination.* Austin, TX: Pro-Ed.

Sander, E. (1972). When are speech sounds learned? *Journal of Speech and Hearing Disorders, 37*(1), 55-63.

Schwartz, H.D. (2012). *A primer on communication and communicative disorders.* Boston, MA: Pearson.

Skinner, B.F. (1957). *Verbal behavior.* East Norwalk, CT: Appleton-Century-Crofts.

Stoel-Gammon, C., & Dunn, C. (1985). *Normal and disordered phonology in children.* Austin, TX: Pro-Ed.

Tomasello, M. (2003). *Constructing a language.* Cambridge, MA: Harvard University Press.

Vygotsky, L.S. (1978). *Mind in society: The development of higher psychological processes.* Cambridge, MA: Harvard University Press.

Acknowledgments

We express our appreciation to:

Faculty and staff of Chapman University, Orange, CA, Communication Sciences and Disorders Program

H.D. Schwartz for inspiring us to create a study guide

Layout and design by Tyler Schwartz
Edited by Linda R. Schreiber

A Cognitive Press/Attainment Company Publication

International Phonetic Alphabet

b	ball	l	lime	t	ten
tʃ	cheese	m	moon	θ	three
d	dog	n	never	ð	them
f	fun	ŋ	wing	v	van
g	good	p	pin	w	warm
h	hug	r	red	j	yarn
dʒ	jug	s	sun	z	zap
k	kind	ʃ	shine	ʒ	measure

i	see	u	zoo	ʌ	sun
ɪ	pin	ʊ	hook	ə	lesson
eɪ	plane	oʊ	go	ɝ	learn
ɛ	red	ɔ	ball	ɚ	butter
æ	lap	ɑ	top	aɪ	buy
ɔɪ	toy	aʊ	shout		

the COGNITIVE *press*

Attainment Company, Inc.

The Cognitive Press
18879 64th Ave.
Chippewa Falls, WI 54729
www.cognitivepress.com
(715) 861-3209

Attainment Company, Inc.
P.O. Box 930160
Verona, WI 53593-0160
www.attainmentcompany.com
(800) 327-4269

ISBN 1-57861-790-1

EVIDENCE-BASED OPTIONS FOR INTERVENTION

Persons with HL or who are deaf respond well to a wide range of interventions as children and adults.

Intervention	Type of HL	Level of Severity	Age and/or Life Factors
Speech-language intervention	C, SN	mild, moderate	All; varies with setting, age, needs, interest
Hearing aids	SN	mild, moderate, severe	All
Assistive listening devices (ALD)	C, SN	mild, moderate, severe	All
Cochlear implant	SN	severe	Implanted as young as possible; later in life, a choice
Lip-reading	SN	moderate	All
Cued speech	SN	moderate, severe	All; dependent on ability to focus attention
Aural rehab	C, SN	moderate	Support as needed throughout life
Auditory-oral (Listening/Speaking)	SN	mild, moderate, severe	Begin very young
Auditory-visual-oral	SN	moderate, severe	When visual cues are needed
Auditory-global	SN	moderate, severe	When even more cues are needed
Manual (ASL)	SN	severe, deaf	When daily access to other signers
Total (signing & speech)	SN	severe, deaf	For young children; a compromise approach
Sign codes, Signed English, Pidgin	SN	severe, deaf	To support ASL; to read and write English
None		mild, moderate, severe	Functions well in life and does not view D/HL as a disability

INTERVENTION

✔ Depends on the age, etiology, type, and degree of hearing loss

✔ Depends upon the preferences and life choices of the individual, family, and community

✔ Chosen intervention may change during the lifetime of the individual and be completely different or no intervention may become appropriate

✔ SLPs and audiologists should thoroughly inform individuals with hearing loss or their families (in the case of newborns and young children) of all options, and provide what the individual chooses

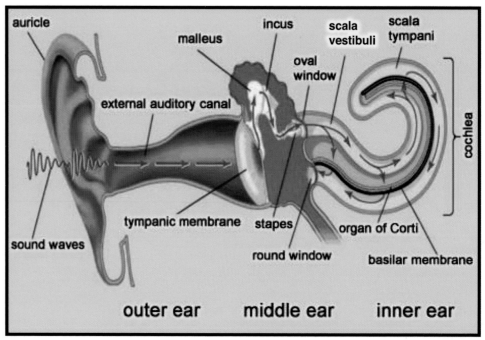

Encyclopedia Britannica Online. (1997). Ear: Hearing mechanism.
Retrieved from http://www.britannica.com/EBchecked/media/536/The-mechanism-of-hearing

Hearing is a sensation, like taste, smell, and touch. Sound is a phenomenon that the human hearing mechanism is designed to perceive. When the hearing mechanism—the ear and the much more extensive neurological tissue hidden within the brain—perceives sound, a person hears.

COMMON CAUSES OF HEARING LOSS

Conductive Middle Ear Problems	Caused by allergies, infections, perforated drum, and blockages in the middle ear; are the leading cause of hearing loss in children and, though transient, may cause significant learning problems during critical times
Sensorineural Losses	The result of genetics, syndromes, viral infections, prematurity, aging, and noise exposure

SPEECH AND LANGUAGE CONCERNS

- ✔ Speech sound and phonological disorders
- ✔ Mild-to-severe language disorders
- ✔ Abnormal voice
- ✔ Academic, social, and vocational challenges

TERMS

Hearing loss: when any portion of the hearing mechanism fails to function, an individual is at risk of hearing loss (HL) or deafness (D)

Hearing mechanism: converts air pressure fluctuations into electrical energy, then propels it swiftly from one brain cell to another to be interpreted as speech and a recognizable code, known as language

Speech: a highly complex sound (300 to 4,000 Hz) perceived by the human ear

Sound: fluctuating air pressure patterns occurring at varying frequencies (pitch) and intensities (volume). Humans are capable of hearing within a fairly narrow band of air pressure—15,000 to 18,000 Hz

TYPES OF HEARING LOSS

Conductive (C) loss: an obstruction in transmission of sound from the external ear; can be transient and can often be corrected

Sensorineural (SN) loss: malfunction of the cochlea or the VIIIth cranial nerve; is a permanent loss

Mixed loss: elements of both types

Auditory processing disorder (APD): pathologies in the hearing centers of the brain, which cause language information to be poorly perceived; may occur when hearing is normal

MEASUREMENT

- ✔ Hearing is measured by an audiologist.

- ✔ Speech-language pathologists may conduct hearing screening or help to interpret audiograms and tympanograms to parents, educational teams, etc.

- ✔ Oto-acoustic emissions (OAE) and auditory brain stem response (ABR) are used to screen newborns for HL.

- ✔ Pure-tone audiometrics (air and bone), tympanometry (movement of the eardrum), and sophisticated inner ear measurements are common and reliable.

- ✔ A battery of tests determines if hearing loss, or perhaps auditory processing, contributes to an individual's speech or language delays/disorders.

TERMS

Aspiration: food or liquid entering the airway

Bolus: a soft mass of chewed food prepared for swallowing

Diverticulum: a pouch that can collect food

Esophagus: the tube that connects the pharynx with the stomach

Fistula: a hole

Pharynx: the throat

ASSESSMENT PROCEDURE

Standard	Specific
Detailed case history Review of medical records Interviews of the patient, family, and related health professionals	Screening of speech, voice, oral language, and written language skills Visual inspection of the oral cavity Testing of cranial nerve function Tests of swallows for varying consistencies of foods and liquids Videofluoroscopic assessment (modified barium swallow) Endoscopy

TREATMENT APPROACHES

Medical Treatment	Behavioral Interventions
Surgical option Alternative feeding route (oral vs. non-oral) Pharmacological management	Adjustment of the food given Alteration of the feeding activity Change of the patient's position Modification of the oral-pharyngeal mechanism through motor exercises, sensory stimulation, and prosthetic adjustments Alteration of the physiology of the swallow

SYMPTOMS

Trouble chewing the bolus, preparing it for swallow, initiating the swallow, propelling the bolus through the pharynx, and passing food to the esophagus

Weight loss or dehydration

Bouts of pneumonia or chest congestion

Liquids or food leaking from the mouth or food getting stuck in the mouth

Extra effort required for swallowing and chewing

Excessive coughing while eating or drinking or immediately after

The presence of a gurgling sound during or after eating or drinking

DYSARTHRIAS

Dysarthria refers to a group of speech disorders resulting from disturbances in muscular control-weakness, slowness, or poor coordination- of the speech mechanism **due to injury to the central and/or peripheral nervous system**. This imperfect articulation actually encompasses **coexisting neurogenic disorders** of one or more of the basic processes of speech: respiration, phonation, resonance, articulation, and prosody.

A **swallowing disorder**—also known as **dysphagia**—involves impairment in the oral, pharyngeal, or esophageal phases of swallowing. Dysphagia can result in poor nutrition or dehydration, embarrassment in social settings, lack of enjoyment when eating or drinking, and can present a risk of aspiration (which could lead to pneumonia or chronic lung disease).

PHASES OF TYPICAL SWALLOWING

1. **Oral preparatory phase**—chewed food is prepared for swallow by forming a bolus.

2. **Oral phase**—the bolus is propelled from the front of the mouth to the back. A combination of the stimulation of the bolus and tongue movements triggers the muscle contractions that begin the next stage when the bolus passes through the anterior faucial arches.

3. **Pharyngeal phase**—airway is closed to prevent material from entering. The upper esophageal sphincter opens to receive the bolus. Bolus is moved from the pharynx to the esophagus by pressure resulting from the tongue base and pharyngeal walls contracting.

4. **Esophageal stage**—muscle contractions move food from the esophagus to the stomach.

DISORDERS ASSOCIATED WITH EACH PHASE

1. Difficulty shaping and managing the bolus.

2. Problems in the movement of the bolus posteriorly; food residue in the oral cavity; reduced range of tongue movement and elevation; and reduced tongue, labial, and buccal strength.

3. Reduced movement of the base of tongue, a delayed or absent swallow reflex, penetration of food in the nasal cavity or airway, aspiration, food residue, and difficulties in propelling the bolus through the pharynx.

4. Reflux of food from the esophagus to the pharynx, difficulty passing the bolus through the cricopharyngeus muscle, and development of atypical features, such as a fistula or diverticulum.

CRANIAL NERVES

CN V	Trigeminal
CN VII	Facial
CN IX	Glossopharyngeal
CN X	Vagus
CN XI	Spinal accessory
CN XII	Hypoglossal

ETIOLOGY

Damage to the nervous system:

• stroke

• traumatic brain injury

• diseases affecting the nervous system (e.g., Parkinson's disease, multiple sclerosis, muscular dystrophy, etc.)

• spinal cord injury

Injury:

• mouth, throat, or esophageal cancer head and neck injury surgical injury

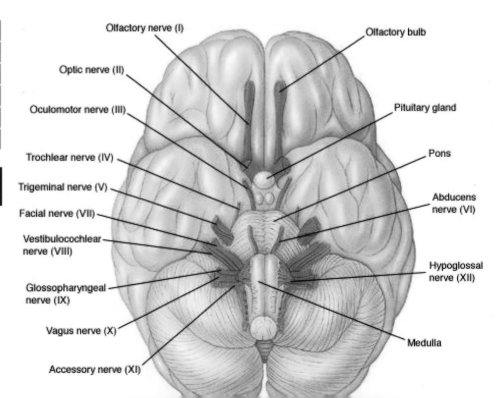

Olfactory nerve (I)
Optic nerve (II)
Oculomotor nerve (III)
Trochlear nerve (IV)
Trigeminal nerve (V)
Facial nerve (VII)
Vestibulocochlear nerve (VIII)
Glossopharyngeal nerve (IX)
Vagus nerve (X)
Accessory nerve (XI)
Olfactory bulb
Pituitary gland
Pons
Abducens nerve (VI)
Hypoglossal nerve (XII)
Medulla

TERMS

Aided communication: using equipment, boards, switches to communicate

Augmentative and alternative communication (AAC): techniques or procedures and processes by which an individual's communication skills are maximized for functional and effective communication; involves supplementing or replacing natural speech and/or writing with aids

High-tech AAC: sophisticated electronic devices with multiple programming options and computer access

Low-tech AAC device: simple-to-program electronic devices

Multimodal AAC: using more than one type of AAC device at one time (e.g., signs, high-tech device, low-tech device, photos, etc.)

No-tech AAC: communicating without a device that is plugged in or uses batteries

Speech-generating device (SGD): a device that produces face-to-face and telephone communication

Unaided communication: using hand signals, signs, gestures, eye gaze, etc. to communicate

Communication modalities is an area of study that examines manual, augmentative, and alternative communication techniques and assistive technologies. These are devices that compensate for temporary or permanent impairments, activity limitations, and participation restrictions of individuals with severe disorders of speech-language production and/or comprehension, including spoken and written modes of communication (ASHA, 2005b).

COMMUNICATION BILL OF RIGHTS

National Joint Committee for the Communication Needs of Persons with Severe Disabilities (1992)

All people are entitled to the following rights in their daily interactions:

- ✔ To request desired objects, actions, events, and people
- ✔ To refuse undesired objects, actions, or events
- ✔ To express personal preferences and feelings
- ✔ To be offered choices and alternatives
- ✔ To reject offered choices
- ✔ To request and receive another person's attention and interaction
- ✔ To ask for and receive information about changes in routine and environment
- ✔ To receive intervention to improve communication skills
- ✔ To have access to AAC at all times

USERS

- ✔ Individuals with severe communication and cognitive impairments

- ✔ Individuals with complex medical and/or daily support needs due to developmental conditions (e.g., autism spectrum disorders, cerebral palsy, apraxia, developmental disabilities, and intellectual disabilities)

- ✔ Individuals with complex medical and/or daily support needs due to acquired conditions (e.g., stroke, traumatic brain injury, Parkinson's disease, dementia, and amyotrophic lateral sclerosis)

- ✔ Individuals who cannot speak or write typically need AAC—everyone has something to say

ASSESSMENT

- ✔ Involves conventional testing when possible with careful observation of the person's physical skills and intent to communicate

- ✔ Often determines that receptive language skills greatly exceed expressive ones, leading to the conclusion that the individual could benefit from a more consistent language output process

- ✔ Examines the potential of using eye gaze, pointing, or assistive technology to indicate communication intent

- ✔ Determines whether individuals need to use pictures, photos, symbols, icons, etc. to represent the meaning items in their lives

- ✔ Determines if the individual can read in order to determine the most appropriate AAC system

INTERVENTION

- ✔ Is intensive and focused on improving life outcomes through enhanced communication

- ✔ Is practiced in natural settings

- ✔ Trains communication partners

- ✔ Selects vocabulary for the AAC system with the client

- ✔ Is highly individualized in the areas of linguistic competence, pragmatics, social language, and the use of operational strategies of the AAC device to engage in conversational turns with others

- ✔ Uses print in AAC systems when appropriate and productive for school, work, and social life activities

Cognitive aspects of communication include attention, memory, problem solving, and executive functioning. Impairment in these areas can result from an acquired brain injury, such as from a stroke or a traumatic brain injury. These impairments result in communication that is less appropriate and effective.

RIGHT HEMISPHERE STROKE

In the majority of people, the left side of the brain controls language, while the right side controls cognitive functioning. In a right hemisphere stroke, damage occurs to the right side of the brain, resulting in impairment in areas of cognitive communication.

TRAUMATIC BRAIN INJURY (TBI)

The impact that a TBI has upon communication depends upon the type of injury sustained, and which parts of the brain were injured. A coup-contracoup injury, as often seen in automotive accidents, results in damage to the frontal and occipital lobes. Damage to the prefrontal cortex specifically can result in impairment in areas of cognitive communication.

TERMS

Attention: selective awareness or responsiveness to a part of the environment; necessary for memory processing

Executive function: a function of the frontal lobes of the brain; includes the skills of goal setting, behavior planning and sequencing, self-monitoring and evaluation of own behavior; helps the individual integrate internal and external stimuli to be sure that behavior (such as communication) is compatible with the context and the individual's needs and intent

Memory: process by which sensations, impressions, and ideas are recalled; involves retention of input for sufficient time to process and store the information

Perception: the conscious mental registration of a sensory stimulus; process of integrating sensory stimuli into meaningful units (Hartley, 1995)

TYPES OF MEMORY

Short-term memory: temporary storage of information lasting a few seconds or minutes

- ✔ Working memory: ability to hold information temporarily while performing mental tasks

Long-term memory: permanent storage of knowledge and experiences over various time periods; divided into several categories

- ✔ **Semantic memory:** memory for knowledge, including meanings of words
- ✔ **Episodic memory:** memory for past experiences
- ✔ **Declarative memory:** memory of events and facts
- ✔ **Procedural memory:** memory for motor and pattern tasks (e.g., riding a bicycle); automatic memory of the sequence of a task

COGNITIVE SKILLS

Reasoning: ability to make inferences and draw conclusions based on known information

Problem solving: a multistep process of

- ✔ recognizing and analyzing a problem
- ✔ developing alternative solutions for solving a problem
- ✔ evaluating solutions
- ✔ selecting the most appropriate solution
- ✔ implementing the solution and evaluating the effectiveness of the solution

Making judgments: forming an opinion or estimate; predicting consequences of an action based on known information; a part of problem solving, helps to select the most appropriate solutions and evaluate effectiveness

Being aware of orientation: awareness of self in relation to person, place, situation, and time; results from interaction of attention, memory, and perception, plus higher cognitive processes

Data from Cherney, Halper, & Burns (1996)

COMPONENTS OF ATTENTION

Focused attention: ability to direct attention to specific sensory stimuli

Sustained attention: actively maintaining attention to stimuli over a period of time

Selective attention: ability to focus attention on target stimuli while ignoring irrelevant stimuli

Alternating attention: ability to shift from one task to another task that requires different mental processes

Divided attention: ability to focus and sustain attention on more than one task simultaneously

Data from Cherney, Halper, & Burns (1996)

APHASIA

Aphasia: an acquired language problem caused by damage to the brain in the hemisphere responsible for communication. It often manifests itself in disorders of attention, execution function, memory, and perception. Stroke is the most common cause; all modes of expressive and receptive communication including speaking, writing, reading, listening, and gesturing can be affected depending on the location in the brain where the stroke occurred and the size of the stroke.

Optimal voice production is based upon intact anatomy and physiology of the larynx and surrounding structures. A voice disorder occurs when part of the voice mechanism is damaged or injured in some way. Persons with severe hearing loss may have a voice disorder because they cannot hear the speech characteristics of others, nor monitor their own voice features.

Vocal Pitch	Vocal Volume	Vocal Quality
✔ Frequency with which the vocal folds vibrate (often described as fundamental frequency) ✔ Fundamental frequency is generally considered an individual's habitual or typical pitch	✔ Perceived intensity, volume, or loudness ✔ Determined by the intensity of the sound signal; the more intense the sound signal, the greater the perceived loudness	✔ Refers to the physical complexity of the laryngeal tone, which is modified by the resonating cavities; the determination of voice quality is subjective

The most common cause of voice disorders is vocal abuse in children or adults

The human voice undergoes certain changes throughout the lifespan; between birth and death everyone experiences voice changes. The most notable change occurs in males during puberty.

Disorders of Resonance

Hypernasality: Occurs when the velopharyngeal mechanism does not close the nasal cavity completely, resulting in air resonating in the nasal cavity.

Hyponasality: Occurs when there is lack of appropriate nasal resonance on nasal sounds /m, n, ŋ/; can occur due to enlarged adenoids or tonsils.

Assimilative Nasality: Usually occurs when the sound from a nasal consonant carries over to the neighboring vowels.

Cul-de-sac Resonance: Occurs when the oral cavity is partially closed at the back and open in front. Some sound waves generated by the larynx are kept from reaching the oral cavity, resulting in distorted voice and resonance; can be caused by enlarged adenoids or tonsils.

Disorders of Phonation

Carcinoma and Laryngectomy: The larynx is a common site of cancer; treatment for the cancer can include surgery, chemotherapy, and radiation. Surgery can consist of total or partial removal of the larynx.

Physically and Neurologically Based Disorders of Phonation

Disorder Resulting from Abuse: Occurs as the result of long- or short-term excessive muscular effort and tension on the part of the vocal folds, which produces vocal nodules, polyps, and contact ulcers.

Disorder of Loudness: Occurs when clients speak too loud or soft as determined by listeners, for a variety of reasons including clinical depression, illness, or psychological trauma.

Disorder of Pitch: Occurs when persons speak with a pitch that is too high or too low for their age and gender.

Data from Roseberry-McKibbin & Hegde (2006)

TERMS DESCRIBING VOICE QUALITY

Hoarseness

Harshness

Strain-Strangle

Breathiness

Glottal fry (heard when the vocal folds vibrate very slowly; resultant sound occurs in slow, but discrete, bursts and is of extremely low pitch resulting in "crackly" voice)

Diplophonia (two pitches are heard at the same time)

Stridency (shrill, unpleasant, somewhat high-pitched and tinny)

Assessment	Treatment
✔ Includes a wide variety of instrumental evaluations ✔ Includes a perceptual evaluation by a speech-language pathologist	✔ Includes collaboration with medical colleagues, vocal rest, and exercises to reduce tension or alter method of voice onset

Data from Roseberry-McKibbin & Hegde (2006)

Fluency disorders are speech disorders. There are two main types of fluency disorders, stuttering and cluttering. Stuttering and cluttering occur in all languages, across all cultures and races, and are not associated with intellectual ability or a specific age group. Stuttering is often defined in terms of characteristics rather than etiology.

FLUENT SPEECH

- **is produced with relative ease**
- **is smooth**
- **is relatively rapid**
- **is rhythmic**
- **does not contain a large number of disfluencies**

ETIOLOGY

- ✔ **Cause of stuttering is unknown**
- ✔ **Appears to be strong evidence for a genetic basis**
- ✔ **Theories/Hypotheses include environmental, genetic, and neurophysiological causes**

ASSESSMENT AND TREATMENT CONSIDERATIONS

Adaptation	Reduction in frequency of stuttering that occurs when a short passage is repeatedly read aloud
Consistency	Occurrence of stuttering on the same word when a passage is repeatedly read aloud
Adjacency	Occurrence of new stuttering on words that surround previously stuttered words
Audience Size	Frequency of stuttering increases with an increase in audience size

DISFLUENT SPEECH

	Examples:
Repetitions	
Part-word repetitions	"W-w-w-Wednesday"
Whole word repetitions	"I-I-I go there"
Phrase repetitions	"I don't... I don't... I don't want to."
Sound prolongations	"Nnnnnnnot that"
Interjections	"Buh-uh-black"
Pauses	[Pause]... "I live there."
Broken words	"Be... [pause] cause she is."
Incomplete sentences	"That car..."
Revisions	That b b b [boy] guy is my friend."

STUTTERING IN YOUNG CHILDREN

Most stuttering begins in children between the ages of 2 and 5 years.

Some young children recover without treatment.

Some children need early intervention to achieve normal fluency.

There are normal periods of disfluency in development. Normal nonfluencies occur in children developing language between the ages of 2 and 4 years.

Stuttering is more likely to occur on function words (articles, conjunctions, prepositions, and pronouns)

STUTTERING IN ADULTS & SCHOOL-AGE CHILDREN

More likely to occur
- ✔ on consonants than on vowels
- ✔ on the first sound or syllable of a word
- ✔ on the first word in a phrase or sentence
- ✔ on the first word in a grammatical clause
- ✔ on longer and less frequently used words
- ✔ on content words (nouns, verbs, adjectives and adverbs)

CLUTTERING

- ✔ Involves rapid repetition of syllables among other disfluencies
- ✔ Involves rapid, disordered articulation resulting in unintelligible speech
- ✔ Can coexist with stuttering
- ✔ Involves abnormally fast or irregular rate, or both

Social communication, or pragmatics,

refers to the use of language within a social context. Pragmatic skills involve knowledge of how, where, when, and with whom language is used. People can be born with difficulties using language socially, or they can experience difficulties as the result of a brain injury. Also, children with a specific language impairment (SLI) can have difficulties with pragmatic aspects of language. Difficulty with social communication is a hallmark of autism spectrum disorders (ASD). Social communication is increasingly recognized as being critical to academic, social, and vocational success.

)) Language context:

- ✔ where the conversation takes place
- ✔ to whom the conversation is directed
- ✔ what and who is present at the time

TERMS

Cohesion: ordering and organizing utterances in a message so they build logically on one another

Communicative intent: an intentional shift of attention between desired object and communication partner

Functional communication: what is being communicated through a person's behavior

Joint attention: awareness of focus on the same object or event as another person

Presuppositional knowledge: a speaker's supposition about the listener's knowledge of the information being discussed

Conversational maxims (Grice, 1975): unspoken rules of conversation involving the quantity, quality, clarity, and relevance of a person's remarks

Theory of Mind: the understanding that other people have viewpoints; allows one to attribute thoughts, desires, and intentions to others; helps to predict actions and outcomes and make inferences

Narrative language is the communication of a series of events that occur over time. Narratives can be evaluated for structure, quality, and content. Analyzing narratives reveals underlying deficits in language function that standardized assessments do not.

Proficient Social Communicators	Individuals with Disordered Social Communication
✔ Provide listeners with adequate information without redundancy	✔ May give too little or too much information
✔ Monitor listeners' reactions for indications of understanding and interest	✔ Have difficulty processing nonverbal cues of conversational partners (e.g., eye contact, gestures, etc.)
✔ Adjust communication based upon the listener's reaction	✔ Generally do not adjust communication based on a conversational partner's nonverbal cues
✔ Make the sequence of statements coherent and logical	✔ May not sequence information in a logical order; may omit important information
✔ Take turns with other speakers	✔ May not give listeners a chance to speak, or may give a delayed response to a conversational partner
✔ Maintain a topic	✔ May change topics inappropriately
✔ Repair communication breakdowns	✔ Might not catch and correct errors made when talking
✔ Develop the ability to make indirect requests	✔ May not make or correctly interpret indirect requests

Language is a rule-based code that we learn from each other to communicate our ideas and needs. It is a complex and dynamic system of agreed-upon symbols used in various modes (e.g., speech, signing, pictures, writing). Each of the 6,000 languages in use in the world has an historical, a social, and a cultural context. A mix of biological, cognitive, psychosocial, and environmental factors determines language learning and use.

Receptive Language

refers to the words, phrases, and sentences an individual understands but does not necessarily produce. It is based on listening and believed to emerge before production. Answering yes/no questions, pointing to a response, or responding using other actions (e.g., eye gazing to an answer) are generally used to assess a person's receptive language skills.

Expressive Language

refers to the speech used by an individual and is measured in all five parameters. Discourse or conversation is the easiest way to analyze this production.

Language is hard-wired in the brain, but the environment must trigger it.

✔ **Some aspects of language are nonlinguistic, such as nonverbal cues, facial expressions, body language, and the socio-cultural roles that individuals all maintain.**

FIVE PARAMETERS OF LANGUAGE

Parameter	Definition	Symptoms of Disorder
Phonology	Rules for speech sounds	Unintelligible speech; deletions, substitutions, or reductions of sounds in patterns
Semantics	Meaning of words	Poor vocabulary, literal (vs. figurative) understanding of words, literacy problems
Syntax	Word order for meaning	Confusing word order in sentences, inappropriate use of wh-questions, short sentences
Morphology	Smallest unit of meaning	Deleted word endings marking plurality or verb tensing
Pragmatics	Use of language	Inappropriate social interaction, poor interpretation of social cues

Theoretical Models of Language Acquisition

The NATURE Perspective	The NURTURE Perspective
✔ Children are born with basic linguistic capacities ✔ Innate capacity is known as: - Language acquisition device (Chomsky) - Syntactic bootstrapping (Gleitman) - Semantic bootstrapping (Pinker)	✔ Suggests that children are born knowing nothing ✔ Language and language is learned through: - Operant conditioning (Skinner) - Social interaction (Vygotsky, Tomasello) - Emerging cognitive development (Piaget)

TERMS

Cognitive referencing: suggests that children cannot perform higher on standardized language tests than their corresponding skill level on standardized cognitive tests. (This has not been proven true, but SLPs are often called upon to explain the distinct differences between language competencies and IQ scores.)

Dialects and second language learning: dialects affect both phonology and syntax of language; these are not disorders. Sometimes adolescents or adults want to modify or change their accents or dialects and seek assistance from an SLP.

Language sample: a universal form of nonstandardized language assessment in which at least 100 utterances are collected/recorded, transcribed, and analyzed to determine critical measurements of expressive language (e.g., mean length of utterance [MLU], communication unit, type-token ratio, narrative language structures, etc.); it can be used to measure all five parameters of language, including prosody, and the results can help determine a disorder or monitor intervention progress.

Naturalistic assessment: a form of assessment whereby the examiner observes and records language reception and production in the daily environment of the individual rather than in a prepared test setting. Both adults and children are more likely to demonstrate their true language skills when interacting in familiar situations or with known persons.

Standard American English (SAE): is the language used in the United States by the media, government, and most businesses. It is taught and modeled in the schools.

Standardized test: a form of assessment that collects norm-referenced data permitting comparison of an individual's performance to a large population of similar individuals. Results are typically reported in standard scores and percentiles.

LANGUAGE DIFFERENCE

SAE may not be the dialect of the individual's home or community.

✔ An individual may use more than one language at home.

✔ An individual may use only one language, but it is not SAE.

✔ Is common and not a sign of disorder (a long, silent period in early language learning; difficulty with code switching; problems in using syntactical structures from an earlier language; and fossilization, in which some error forms continue no matter how fluent the person becomes).

If a disorder is suspected, assess the individual in his or her own language or with the close assistance of a

PLACE-MANNER-VOICING

A classification system of consonant speech sounds according to place of articulation, manner of production, and presence or lack of voicing.

Place	Manner	Voicing
bilabial	stop	voiced
dental (interdental)	fricative	voiceless
labiodental	affricate	
alveolar	nasal	
palatal	liquid	
velar	glide	
glottal		

Phonological Patterns

Processes Disappearing by 3 Years

Process	Description	Example
Unstressed syllable deletion	Omitting a weak syllable	banana → /nænə/
Final consonant deletion	Omitting a singleton consonant at the end of a word	cat → /kæ/
Diminutization	Adding /i/ at the end of nouns	dog → /dagi/
Velar fronting	Substituting a front sound for a back sound	can → /tæn/
Consonant assimilation	Changing a phoneme so it takes on a characteristic of another sound in the word	cat → /tæt/
Reduplication	Repeating phonemes or syllables	bottle → /bɔbɔ/
Prevocalic voicing	Substituting a voiced consonant for a voiceless consonant before a vowel	sun → /zʌn/

Data from Stoel-Gammon & Dunn (1985)

Processes Persisting after 3 Years

Process	Description	Example
Cluster reduction	Omitting one or more consonants in a sequence of consonants	clean → /kin/
Epenthesis	Adding a sound, typically /ʌ/, between two consonants	black → /bʌlæk/
Gliding	Substituting /w/ or /j/ for another consonant	run → /wʌn/
Vocalization/ Vowelization	Substituting a vowel for a consonant	car → /kə/
Stopping	Substituting a stop consonant for a fricative, liquid, nasal, or glide	sun → /dʌn/
Depalatalization	Substituting a nonpalatal consonant for a palatal consonant	shy → /saɪ/
Final consonant devoicing	Substituting a voiceless final consonant for a voiced consonant	bag → /bæk/

Data from Stoel-Gammon & Dunn (1985)

A review of studies that determined the age by which at least 75% of children no longer use a given process

Individual Process	Description	Example	Likely Age of Disappearance
Denasalization	Changing a nasal consonant to a nonnasal	mat → /bæt/	2.6
Assimilation	Changing a phoneme so it takes on a characteristic of another sound in the word	cat → /tæt/	3
Affrication	Substituting an affricate for a nonaffricate	sheep → /tʃip/	3
Final consonant deletion	Omitting a singleton consonant at the end of a word	cat → /kæ/	3
Fronting of initial velar singles	Substituting a front sound for a back sound	can → /tæn/	4
Deaffrication	Replacing an affricate with a continuant or stop	chip → /sɪp/	4
Cluster reduction (without /s/)	Omitting one or more consonants in a sequence of consonants	grape → /gep/	4
Depalatalization of final singles	Substituting a nonpalatal for a palatal sound at the end of a word	dish → /dɪt/	4.6
Depalatalization of initial singles	Substituting a nonpalatal for a palatal sound at the beginning of a word	shy → /taɪ/	5
Alveolarization	Substituting an alveolar for a nonalveolar sound	chew → /tu/	5
Final consonant devoicing	Substituting a voiceless final consonant for a voiced consonant	bag → /bæk/	5
Cluster reduction (with /s/)	Omitting /s/ in the initial position of a cluster	step → /tɛp/	5
Labialization	Replacing nonlabial sound with a labial sound	tan → /pæn/	6
Initial voicing	Substituting a voiced consonant for a voiceless consonant before a vowel	sun → /zʌn/	6
Gliding of initial liquids	Substituting a voiced consonant for a voiceless consonant before a vowel	run → /wʌn/	7
Epenthesis	Adding a sound between two consonants	black → /bʌlæk/	8

Data from Peña-Brooks & Hegde (2007)

Speech Sounds

AGE

Sounds listed top to bottom with bars spanning ages from 2 to 8:

- p (2–3)
- m (2–3)
- h (2–3)
- n (2–3)
- w (2–3)
- b (2–3.5)
- k (2.5–4)
- g (2.5–4)
- d (2.5–4)
- t (3–6)
- ng (3–4)
- f (2.5–4)
- y (2.5–4)
- r (3–5)
- l (3–6)
- s (3–8)
- ch (3.5–7)
- sh (3.5–7)
- z (3.5–7)
- j (4–7)
- v (4–7)
- voiceless th (4.5–5.5)
- voiced th (5–5.5)
- zh (6–8.5)

Bar starts at median age at which children produce the sound and extends to age at which 90% of children produce the sound.

From "When Are Speech Sounds Learned" by E.K. Sander, 1972, Journal of Speech and Hearing Disorders, 37, p. 62. © 1972 by the American Speech-Language-Hearing Association. Reprinted with permission.

Articulation disorders may affect a person's social-emotional well-being, life work, and interpersonal relations. Because articulation is visible and audible, it can provoke negative judgments and reactions. While phonological disorders are recognized as language-based impairments, they are generally studied and treated alongside articulation disorders and so are included here.

TERMS

Articulation disorder: sound substitutions, distortions, and omissions; difficulty producing specific, individual speech sounds

Phonetics: description and classification of speech sounds

Phonology: patterns of phonemes that occur in a language

Phonotactics: description of allowed combinations of phonemes in a particular language

Phonological disorder: a language-based disorder in which a person has difficulty organizing speech sounds into a system of contrasts, resulting in error patterns

OLLER'S STAGES (1980) OF PRELINGUISTIC DEVELOPMENT

Phase 1: Phonation (0:0-0:1)—reflexive vocalizations, produced with a relatively closed mouth, dominate.

Phase 2: Cooing (0:2-0:3)—velar and uvular consonant and back vowel-like sounds are produced; "primitive syllables" may be perceived but there is no timing element.

Phase 3: Expansion (0:4-0:6)—vocal play is predominant with a wide variety of productions, includes squeals, yells, and vowels. Some CV sequences are produced, but tend to be slow and irregular in timing and are not canonical syllables. Infants show increasing control over vocal mechanisms.

Phase 4: Reduplicated Babbling (0:7-0:09)— the beginning of canonical babbling; CV syllables are produced with a true consonant (C) and fully resonant vowel (V). The same CV is repeated multiple times. Sounds produced are primarily stops, nasals, and glides, with place of articulation being primarily bilabial and alveolar. Vowels are typically lax.

Phase 5: Variegated Babbling (0:10-1:0)—CV syllables are produced with various consonants and vowels; variegated syllables are produced with adult-like prosody.

4 BASIC PROCESSES INVOLVED IN SPEECH PRODUCTION

Respiration—the energy source for speech production. Composed of the lungs, bronchi, trachea; the larynx; air passageways of the pharynx, the nose, and sometimes the mouth; rib cage; and diaphragm and associated structure

Phonation—the sound source for all speech sounds, except for voiceless consonants; produced by the vocal folds of the larynx

Articulation—the shaping source for speech sounds, produced by moveable and immovable articulators within the vocal tract

Resonation—the amplification source of speech production, produced by modifying the voiced breath stream and/or damping certain frequency components of the speech sounds. The three resonating cavities are pharyngeal, oral, and nasal.

EXAMPLE EVIDENCE-BASED TREATMENT APPROACHES: ARTICULATION DISORDERS

Phonetic Placement Approach (Articulator Placement)	Prompt (Tactile-Kinesthetic)	Stimulus (Traditional)	Paired Stimuli (Phonetic Context)	Programmed Instruction (Behavior Modification)	Stimulability Enhancement (Stimulability)
Direct instruction in specific placement of articulators to produce specific speech sounds	Use of multi-dimensional tactile prompts to guide articulators in speech sound production	Auditory training and production practice of target in increasing levels of linguistic complexity	Key words paired with words with the target sound produced incorrectly in all contexts	Specification of stimuli, client responses, and consequences (reinforcement, punishment, and differential reinforcement) in small sequential steps	Production of consonants in isolation or CV to increase the number of stimulable sounds

EVIDENCE-BASED TREATMENT APPROACHES: PHONOLOGY

Distinctive Feature	Phonological Cycling	Meaningful Minimal Contrasting Pairs	Maximal Opposition	Nonlinear
Production of contrasting exemplar phonemes, one containing the feature and the other not containing the feature	Phonological patterns are targeted in words containing exemplar sounds in rotating time cycles	Phonological patterns are targeted in contrasting word pairs, one containing the targeted pattern and the other not containing the pattern	Production of contrasting word pairs, differing in multiple phonetic features, increasing the phonetic inventory and complexity level	Various segmental and syllable/word structure levels are targeted through the production of exemplar words for a specified time period

COMMUNICATION SCIENCES AND DISORDERS

QUICK REFERENCE

BY **JUDY MONTGOMERY, PhD, CCC-SLP,** IN COLLABORATION WITH **LAURA MARSHALL, MS**

Communication Sciences and Disorders

is also referred to as speech-language pathology. Professionals who work in this field are speech-language pathologists (SLPs) with a master's degree, or they can be speech-language pathology assistants (SLPAs) with an associate of arts degree or equivalent. A critical aspect of communication is hearing. Audiology, the parallel profession of hearing science, is integrated throughout the field of study.

This guide is designed to increase your understanding of the speech-language profession, to recognize the important aspects of the practice, and to help you apply the information to exam preparation. It is divided into the nine disorder areas identified by the accrediting agency, the American Speech-Language-Hearing Association (ASHA). The nine disorder areas are: articulation; receptive and expressive language; fluency; hearing; voice and resonance; swallowing; cognitive aspects of communication; social aspects of communication; and communication modalities. Speech-language services are delivered in schools, hospitals, private practices, early childhood education programs, university clinics, and homes. Services are provided throughout the human lifespan.

WHAT'S INCLUDED:

1. **Articulation/Phonology**
2. **Receptive and Expressive Language**
3. **Social Communication**
4. **Fluency**
5. **Voice & Resonance**
6. **Cognitive Communication**
7. **Communication Modalities**
8. **Swallowing**
9. **Hearing**

TERMS

What Is Assessment?

SLPs diagnose the nine disorder areas by conducting a thorough evaluation of an individual's speech, language, and communication skills. This includes, but is not limited to, conducting or reviewing developmental history, medical reports, parent/family surveys, standardized and nonstandardized tests, an oral-peripheral exam, a language sample, and audio or video recordings. Most assessments are enhanced with cross-disciplinary input.

What Is Intervention?

Intervention, also referred to as treatment or remediation, is a planned course of action to reduce or eliminate the disorder that was diagnosed as a result of the assessment.

What Is Evidence-Based Practice (EBP)?

EBP is an approach in which high-quality research evidence is integrated with practitioner expertise and client preferences and values into the process of making clinical decisions (ASHA, 2005). Using EBP, both assessment and intervention are designed based on literature and research in the profession.

SPEECH MECHANISM

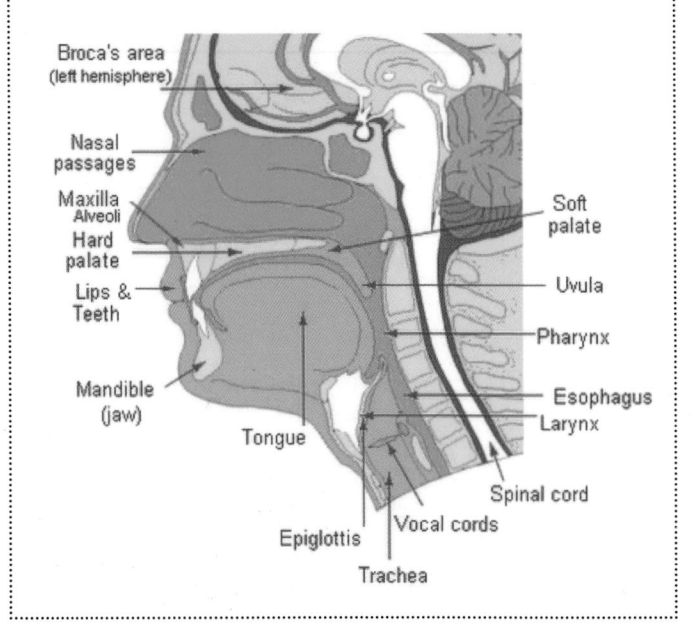

Broca's area (left hemisphere)
Nasal passages
Maxilla Alveoli
Hard palate
Lips & Teeth
Mandible (jaw)
Tongue
Epiglottis
Vocal cords
Trachea
Soft palate
Uvula
Pharynx
Esophagus
Larynx
Spinal cord

Source: www.ling.fju.edu